MAGIC

The Enchanted Himalayas

By Harry Holland

TABLE OF CONTENTS

CHAPTER 1: THE MYSTICAL LAND OF TIBET

In the heart of the majestic Himalayas lies a land shrouded in mystery and enchantment—the captivating realm of Tibet. Nestled between towering mountains and vast plateaus, Tibet has long been revered as a spiritual haven and a sanctuary for seekers of truth. Its unique blend of culture, spirituality, and magic has fascinated travelers and mystics for centuries.

Tibetan culture is rich and vibrant, steeped in ancient traditions that have been passed down through generations. The Tibetan people hold deep reverence for their spiritual heritage, and their devotion to the teachings of Buddhism has shaped the fabric of their society. Within this tapestry of beliefs and practices, Tibetan magic finds its roots.

Magic in Tibet is not merely a collection of spells and illusions; it is an intricate system that interweaves with the very essence of Tibetan spirituality. The Tibetan people understand that magic is not separate from their daily lives but rather an integral part of their existence—a means of connecting with the divine and unlocking the dormant powers within.

Within the pages of this book, "Tibetan Magic: The Enchanted Himalayas," we embark on a transformative journey to explore the depths of Tibetan magical practices. Our voyage will take us through the realms of inner energies, elemental forces, past lives, and profound self-mastery. Together, we will unveil the secrets that have been safeguarded by generations of Tibetan masters, passing down their wisdom from teacher to student.

As we delve into the chapters ahead, we will encounter remarkable practices that harness the power of the mind, body, and spirit. We will discover the ancient technique of Tumo, igniting the inner fire to stimulate the chakras and energy channels, enabling us to withstand the harshest of cold and enhancing our vitality.

Through the practice of entering light trance states, we will trace the threads of our past lives, gaining profound insights into our karmic patterns and the interconnectedness of our souls throughout time.

The power of sound and rhythm will be unveiled, showing us how chanting, drumming, and the harmonious play of vibrations can manipulate energies and create transformative experiences.

Dream Yoga, a spiritual practice that unlocks the hidden potential of our dreams, will open the doors to expanded consciousness, allowing us to navigate the realms of the subconscious with clarity and purpose.

Venturing into the realm of elemental magic, we will dance with the forces of nature, unraveling the techniques that connect us to the profound wisdom and energy of earth, air, fire, and water.

The Four Portals, mystical gateways to the divine, will beckon us to explore their significance and the paths they offer toward higher realms of consciousness.

We will immerse ourselves in the exploration of Siddhis, extraordinary powers that transcend the limits of the physical world, and discover the elaborate magical rites and practices that lead us toward their attainment.

Our journey will also take us through the darker realms as we delve into the ancient and mysterious world of Bonpa Shamanism, unraveling its necromantic practices and understanding its historical significance in Tibetan culture.

We will learn the art of thought forms, creating mental visualizations to manifest the mind's creations and exploring the purpose and potential of these powerful entities known as tulpas.

Glimpses into higher realms will unfold before our eyes as we investigate the phenomenon of visions, their role in spiritual growth, and the profound personal insights they offer.

Through the chapters on self-mastery, we will examine the profound practice of physical yoga, harmonizing our bodies, minds, and spirits, and unlocking the ancient techniques of controlling the body's heat mechanism.

Breathing exercises will serve as gateways to the divine, deepening our spiritual practice, and expanding our consciousness.

We will unravel the mystical art of sending messages on the wind, transcending physical boundaries and connecting with higher realms, guided by the winds that carry our intentions.

In the realm of Tara, the compassionate goddess, we will immerse ourselves, understanding her significance in Tibetan culture and exploring the practices that allow us to connect with her wisdom and grace.

As we conclude our magical journey through the secrets of Himalayan magic, we will reflect on the path unveiled, summarizing the key teachings and sharing personal insights gained along the way.

In the chapters that follow, we will explore how to integrate magic into our daily lives, fostering personal growth and spiritual development by incorporating these profound practices into our routines.

Throughout this journey, we will emphasize the importance of respecting Tibetan culture, traditions, and the sacred knowledge shared within this book, honoring the sacred teachings that have been entrusted to us.

This book is not the end but the beginning of a never-ending quest. It is an invitation for you, dear reader, to embrace your own magical path, to explore the realms of Tibetan magic and spirituality, and to continue your personal journey of discovery and transformation.

So, let us embark on this enchanting adventure together, guided by the wisdom of the Himalayas and the ancient traditions that have been carried through the mists of time. The enchanted land of Tibet awaits us, ready to reveal its secrets and awaken the magic within us all.

CHAPTER 2: TUMO: IGNITING THE INNER FIRE

In the high altitudes of the Himalayas, where the air is thin and the cold bites at the bones, the Tibetan people have discovered a remarkable technique known as Tumo—a practice that allows them to ignite the inner fire within their bodies. Tumo is a profound method of harnessing the power of our inner energies, stimulating the chakras and energy channels that flow throughout our being, and ultimately enabling us to resist extreme cold and enhance our vitality.

To understand the practice of Tumo, we must first recognize the vital role of the subtle energy system in Tibetan magic. According to Tibetan tradition, the body is not merely a physical vessel but a complex interplay of energies that flow through channels called nadis. These nadis intersect at energy centers known as chakras, which serve as gateways to access and manipulate our inner energies.

Through Tumo, we learn to awaken and direct these energies, tapping into the dormant power within ourselves. The practice begins with mastering the breath—a fundamental tool in Tibetan magic. By controlling the breath, we can regulate the flow of energy and awaken the inner fire.

One of the foundational Tumo practices is the Breath of Fire. To practice this technique, sit in a comfortable position, spine erect, and close your eyes. Take a deep inhale through the nose, filling your lungs, and then exhale forcefully through the nose while simultaneously pumping your abdomen inwards. As you exhale, imagine that you are blowing on the embers of a fire, stoking its flames. Repeat this process rapidly, maintaining a steady rhythm.

As you continue the Breath of Fire, focus your attention on the region below the navel, known as the lower Dan Tien. Visualize a flame flickering within this energetic center, growing brighter and more intense with each breath. Feel the warmth spreading throughout your body, revitalizing your cells and awakening your inner fire.

With regular practice, the Tumo technique allows us to withstand extreme cold by generating intense heat within our bodies. Tibetan yogis have been known to perform remarkable feats, such as meditating outdoors in freezing temperatures while wearing nothing more than a simple cloth, their bodies enveloped in the warmth of their inner fire.

Beyond its physical benefits, Tumo serves as a gateway to the deeper realms of consciousness. The awakened inner fire purifies the subtle energy channels, clearing blockages and facilitating the free flow of energy throughout the body. As the energy flows unimpeded, it nourishes our spiritual growth and enhances our connection to the divine.

Practical Example: Let us imagine a practitioner named Kalden who embarks on the practice of Tumo. Every morning, Kalden sets aside a dedicated time for his Tumo practice. Sitting in a serene corner of his room, he assumes a comfortable posture and begins by focusing on his breath, gradually entering into a meditative state.

With each breath, Kalden visualizes the flame of his inner fire growing brighter and more vibrant. He feels the warmth spreading from his lower Dan Tien, enveloping his entire body. As he continues the Breath of Fire, Kalden's senses sharpen, and he becomes acutely aware of the energy flowing within him.

Over time, Kalden notices the transformative effects of Tumo in his daily life. He finds that he is more resistant to the cold weather, feeling a comforting warmth emanating from within him. His vitality and stamina increase, allowing him to engage in physical activities with newfound vigor.

Beyond the physical changes, Kalden experiences a profound spiritual connection. The awakened inner fire opens doorways to higher realms of consciousness, deepening his meditative practices and expanding his awareness of the interconnectedness of all things.

Through the practice of Tumo, we tap into the reservoirs of energy that lie dormant within us, igniting the inner fire that fuels our physical, mental, and spiritual well-being. It is a practice that awakens our potential, enabling us to endure the harshest conditions and connect with the vast realms of the divine within and around us. As we continue our journey through the enchanted Himalayas, let us explore further the threads of past lives and the transformative power of harmony through sound and rhythm.

CHAPTER 3: TRACING THE THREADS OF PAST LIVES

In the tapestry of our existence, the threads of past lives weave a complex and intricate pattern. Tibetan magic offers a doorway to explore these threads, delving into the depths of our consciousness to recall past lives and gain insight into karmic patterns that shape our present reality. Tracing the threads of past lives is a practice that invites us to enter light trance states, where the boundaries of time and space blur, and the secrets of our previous incarnations unfold.

The belief in reincarnation is deeply ingrained in Tibetan culture and spirituality. It is believed that our souls journey through multiple lives, carrying the imprints of past experiences, lessons, and unresolved karmic debts. By accessing the memories of our past lives, we gain a broader perspective on our present circumstances and can take steps to heal, grow, and break free from repetitive patterns.

The practice of tracing past lives begins with entering a state of deep relaxation and heightened awareness. Find a quiet and comfortable space where you can sit or lie down. Close your eyes and take slow, deep breaths, allowing your body and mind to relax. As your breathing becomes rhythmic, imagine yourself descending into a peaceful and serene inner landscape, a sanctuary for exploration.

Once in this state of relaxation, set the intention to connect with your past lives. Visualize a staircase leading downwards, representing a descent into the depths of your subconscious. Step onto the staircase, feeling each step anchoring you deeper into your inner world.

As you descend, you may begin to experience flashes of images, emotions, or sensations from past lives. Allow these impressions to arise naturally, without judgment or analysis. You may see glimpses of different time periods, cultures, or landscapes. You might encounter familiar faces or places that resonate deeply within you.

Pay attention to the emotions that arise as you witness these scenes from the past. Notice if there are recurring themes, relationships, or unresolved conflicts. These glimpses provide valuable insights into the karmic patterns that continue to influence your present life.

Practical Example: Let us imagine a practitioner named Maya who embarks on the journey of tracing her past lives. Maya sets aside a dedicated time for this practice, creating a serene space in her home. She sits comfortably, closes her eyes, and begins her relaxation ritual, focusing on her breath and letting go of any tension.

In her relaxed state, Maya envisions herself standing at the top of a staircase, ready to descend into her subconscious. Step by step, she moves downwards, feeling a sense of calm and anticipation building within her.

As Maya reaches the bottom of the staircase, she finds herself in a lush, green meadow. She walks through the meadow, surrounded by vibrant flowers and gentle breezes. Suddenly, a scene unfolds before her eyes—a bustling marketplace in an ancient city. She feels a deep connection to the place, as if she has been there before.

As Maya continues her exploration, she encounters other vivid scenes—a serene temple nestled in the mountains, a tumultuous battlefield where emotions run high, and a peaceful seaside village where she feels a profound sense of belonging. Each glimpse brings forth a range of emotions, insights, and a greater understanding of her present self.

Over time, Maya notices patterns emerging in her past life

memories. She recognizes recurring relationships, lessons, and themes that parallel her current experiences. These revelations deepen her understanding of her own journey and offer her the opportunity to heal past wounds and make conscious choices in the present.

Tracing the threads of past lives is a transformative practice that opens the door to self-discovery, self-compassion, and personal growth. It reminds us that our existence extends far beyond the boundaries of a single lifetime and invites us to embrace the richness of our collective soul's journey.

In the next chapter, we will explore the power of sound, rhythm, chanting, and drumming in manipulating energies and creating transformative experiences. Join me as we unravel the mysteries of harmony through sound and rhythm in the enchanted Himalayas.

CHAPTER 4: HARMONY THROUGH SOUND AND RHYTHM

In the enchanted Himalayas, sound and rhythm hold the power to transcend the ordinary and awaken the extraordinary. Tibetan magical practices have long recognized the profound influence of sound vibrations on the human energy field and consciousness. In this chapter, we unveil the transformative potential of sound, rhythm, chanting, and drumming, offering you a gateway to manipulate energies and create experiences of harmony and alignment.

Sound is a fundamental force that permeates the universe. Every sound, from the gentle whisper of a breeze to the resounding chant of a mantra, carries its own unique vibration. When we align ourselves with the right sounds and rhythms, we can harmonize our energies and connect with higher realms of consciousness.

Chanting is one such practice that allows us to harness the power of sound. By uttering sacred syllables and mantras, we invoke specific energies and attune ourselves to their vibrations. The repetition of these sounds creates a resonance within us, activating dormant energies and aligning our chakras and energy channels.

Practical Example: Imagine a practitioner named Keshav who seeks to experience the transformative power of sound and rhythm. Keshav begins his practice by finding a quiet and serene space in nature, where he can connect deeply with the elements. He sits comfortably, focusing on his breath and grounding himself in the present moment.

As Keshav enters a state of calmness and centeredness, he takes a deep breath and utters the sacred mantra "Om" with intention and devotion. With each repetition, the sound reverberates within him, awakening his energy centers and invoking a sense of deep resonance. Keshav feels a subtle shift in his energy field, as if the mantra is aligning his inner being with the cosmic vibrations of the universe.

Inspired by the transformative power of chanting, Keshav explores the rhythmic beats of a drum. He selects a traditional Tibetan drum known as a "damaru" and begins to play it with a steady and deliberate rhythm. As the drumbeats fill the air, Keshav enters a state of entrainment, where his heartbeat synchronizes with the rhythmic pulsations of the drum. In this harmonious union of sound and rhythm, he experiences a heightened sense of awareness and connection to the spiritual realm.

The magic of sound and rhythm extends beyond individual practices. In Tibetan rituals and ceremonies, groups of practitioners come together to create a symphony of sacred sounds. They chant mantras, play instruments, and engage in collective drumming, creating a powerful energetic field that amplifies their intentions and prayers.

Through the exploration of sound and rhythm, we learn to attune ourselves to the harmonies of the universe. We discover that our voices and the vibrations we create have the power to heal, transform, and manifest our intentions. By incorporating sound-based practices into our lives, we can cultivate a deep sense of harmony, balance, and alignment with the mystical forces that surround us.

In the next chapter, we will explore the realm of Dream Yoga, where the hidden potential of dreams becomes a gateway to expanded consciousness. Join me as we embark on this journey of awakening the subconscious in the enchanting realm of the Himalayas.

CHAPTER 5: DREAM YOGA: AWAKENING THE SUBCONSCIOUS

In the realm of dreams, the veil between the conscious and the unconscious dissolves, opening a gateway to profound insights, spiritual growth, and expanded consciousness. Dream Yoga, a spiritual practice deeply rooted in Tibetan tradition, allows us to explore the hidden realms of our subconscious mind and harness the transformative power of our dreams. In this chapter, we will embark on a journey of self-discovery, unlocking the hidden potential of our dreams and unraveling the mysteries that lie within.

Dreams have long been regarded as a sacred realm, a landscape where the ordinary and the extraordinary intertwine. Tibetan masters have recognized that the dream state provides a unique opportunity to access deeper layers of consciousness and gain valuable insights into our lives. Through the practice of Dream Yoga, we can cultivate awareness within the dream state, enabling us to navigate, influence, and learn from our dreams.

Practical Example: Let us explore the story of Pema, a devoted practitioner who seeks to unlock the transformative potential of Dream Yoga. Pema begins her practice by establishing a consistent dream journal. Every morning upon waking, she takes a few moments to recall her dreams and record them in her journal. By consistently documenting her dreams, Pema develops a deeper connection to her dream experiences, allowing patterns and symbolism to emerge.

To enhance her dream recall and cultivate lucidity, Pema practices reality checks throughout her waking hours. She frequently questions her reality, asking herself, "Am I dreaming?" and performs simple tests like looking at her hands or trying to float in the air. By incorporating these reality checks into her daily routine, Pema develops a habit of questioning her waking state, which naturally carries over into her dream state.

As Pema's dream recall improves, she begins to explore techniques to induce lucid dreaming. One such technique involves setting intentions before sleep. Pema takes a few moments before bed to reflect on her intentions for the dream state, such as gaining insight into a specific question or seeking guidance on a particular issue. By setting these intentions, she creates a bridge between her conscious mind and her dream state, increasing the likelihood of lucidity and purposeful dreaming.

Once Pema achieves lucidity within a dream, she begins to explore the dream landscape with curiosity and intention. She engages in practices such as visualization, mantra recitation, and energy work within the dream, knowing that the dream state is a malleable realm where intentions manifest swiftly. Pema discovers that by consciously directing her thoughts and emotions within the dream, she can influence the dream's unfolding and gain deeper insights into her subconscious mind.

Through her practice of Dream Yoga, Pema gradually gains access to the vast reservoir of wisdom hidden within her dreams. She discovers that her dreams hold symbolic messages, unresolved emotions, and glimpses of her soul's journey. As she integrates the insights gained from her dreams into her waking life, she experiences profound personal growth and a deepening connection to her true self.

Dream Yoga invites us to approach our dreams with reverence and curiosity, recognizing them as valuable sources of guidance and self-discovery. By exploring the realm of dreams, we can awaken to the limitless potential within us, expand our consciousness, and navigate our spiritual path with greater clarity and insight.

In the next chapter, we will embark on a journey into the world of elemental magic, unraveling the techniques that allow us to dance with the elements and tap into their profound connection with human consciousness. Join me as we explore the enchanting realm where earth, air, fire, and water intertwine in harmony and power.

CHAPTER 6: DANCING WITH THE ELEMENTS

Within the intricate tapestry of creation, the elements - earth, air, fire, and water - hold immense power and wisdom. Tibetan mystical traditions have long recognized the profound connection between the elements and human consciousness. In this chapter, we will embark on a journey to unravel the techniques of elemental magic, inviting you to dance with the elements and tap into their inherent magic.

The elements are not merely external forces; they are woven into the very fabric of our being. Each element possesses unique qualities and symbolism that correspond to different aspects of our lives and consciousness. By developing a conscious relationship with the elements, we can harness their energies to create transformation, healing, and spiritual growth.

Practical Example: Let us meet Tenzin, an aspiring practitioner who seeks to deepen his connection with the elements. Tenzin begins his exploration by dedicating time to immerse himself in nature, observing the manifestations of the elements around him. He walks barefoot on the earth, feeling its stability and grounding energy infusing his body and spirit. He listens to the whispers of the wind, feeling the gentle touch of air against his skin and allowing it to clear his mind. He gazes into the dancing flames of a bonfire, sensing the transformative power and inspiration of fire. Finally, he sits by a flowing river, surrendering to the fluidity and emotional depth of water. Through this conscious immersion, Tenzin establishes a deeper connection with the elements and begins to recognize their presence within him.

To further cultivate his relationship with the elements, Tenzin explores elemental rituals and practices. For earth, he creates an altar adorned with stones and plants, representing the stability and fertility of the earth element. He performs grounding exercises, such as standing barefoot on the earth and visualizing roots growing from his feet, anchoring him to the solid foundation of the earth.

For air, Tenzin engages in mindful breathing exercises, consciously drawing in the vital life force carried by the air and releasing any stagnant energies with each exhale. He practices deep breathing while envisioning himself merging with the vastness of the sky, allowing the expansiveness of air to inspire his thoughts and creativity.

To connect with the element of fire, Tenzin kindles a small fire in a ceremonial setting. He gazes into the flames, meditating on the transformative power of fire and envisioning his intentions being ignited and carried aloft by its energy. He uses fire as a tool for purification, releasing any negative or limiting beliefs into the transformative embrace of the flames.

Finally, for water, Tenzin immerses himself in the healing qualities of water. He takes ritual baths infused with sacred herbs and essential oils, envisioning the water washing away emotional blockages and revitalizing his spirit. He also spends time near bodies of water, engaging in gentle movements and reflecting upon the ebb and flow of his emotions.

As Tenzin deepens his practice of elemental magic, he experiences a profound shift in his connection to the world around him. He realizes that the elements are not separate from him but are a part of his very essence. By engaging in rituals, meditations, and practices that honor the elements, he taps into their transformative power and experiences a harmonious integration of his own elemental nature.

Through the exploration of elemental magic, we awaken to the interplay between our inner and outer worlds. We recognize that by embracing the elements, we embrace the essential aspects of ourselves and gain access to their wisdom, vitality, and transformative potential. In the next chapter, we will venture

HARRY HOLLAND

into the mystical realm of the Four Portals, unlocking gateways to the divine and expanding our consciousness to higher realms of awareness. Join me as we unravel the sacred mysteries that await us.

CHAPTER 7: THE FOUR PORTALS: GATEWAYS TO THE DIVINE

In the realm of Tibetan magic, there exists a profound understanding of the interconnectedness between the earthly and the divine. The Four Portals, also known as the Gateways to the Divine, hold immense mystical significance in Tibetan spirituality. These portals serve as bridges between our ordinary perception and the realms of higher consciousness, offering us access to profound wisdom, spiritual growth, and transformative experiences. In this chapter, we will unveil the secrets of the Four Portals and explore their role in opening doors to divine realms.

The Four Portals represent different aspects of our existence and provide pathways for transcending the limitations of the physical world. Each portal is associated with specific elements, symbolism, and practices that enable us to connect with higher realms of consciousness.

The First Portal: The Portal of Earth
The Portal of Earth represents stability, grounding, and the solid foundation of our physical existence. It is through this portal that we learn to harmonize our earthly nature with the spiritual dimensions. Practices associated with the First Portal include meditation on the qualities of the earth element, connecting with the energy of sacred mountains, and cultivating a deep sense of rootedness within ourselves.

Practical Example: Picture Lhamo, a dedicated practitioner, embarking on a pilgrimage to Mount Kailash, a sacred mountain in Tibet. As Lhamo ascends the mountain, she tunes into the subtle vibrations of the earth beneath her feet, allowing its grounding energy to flow through her. With each step, she visualizes herself becoming one with the mountain, merging her consciousness with the ancient wisdom it holds. By immersing herself in the energy of the First Portal, Lhamo experiences a profound sense of stability, connection, and reverence for the earth.

The Second Portal: The Portal of Air
The Portal of Air represents freedom, expansion, and the realm of thoughts and ideas. It is through this portal that we explore the power of the mind and its capacity to transcend boundaries. Practices associated with the Second Portal include breathwork, visualization techniques, and engaging in contemplative practices that expand the horizons of our perception.

Practical Example: Let us imagine Tashi, a curious seeker, practicing pranayama, the art of breath control. Tashi sits in a serene space, focusing on the inhalation and exhalation of the breath. With each breath, Tashi envisions the air entering his body as a carrier of vital life force and inspiration. He imagines his breath reaching far beyond his physical body, connecting him to the vastness of the sky and the realm of possibilities. Through the exploration of the Second Portal, Tashi discovers the power of his thoughts and gains insights that transcend the confines of ordinary perception.

The Third Portal: The Portal of Fire
The Portal of Fire symbolizes transformation, passion, and the illumination of consciousness. It is through this portal that we awaken the fiery essence within us and ignite the flames of spiritual realization. Practices associated with the Third Portal include working with the transformative power of fire, engaging in ceremonial rituals, and cultivating inner alchemy.

Practical Example: Imagine Dawa, a devoted practitioner, participating in a fire ceremony known as a "fire puja." Dawa sits before a sacred fire, offering prayers and intentions into the flames. As the fire consumes the offerings, Dawa visualizes the purification and transformation of his being, releasing what no longer serves him and invoking the presence of divine light.

Through the exploration of the Third Portal, Dawa experiences a profound sense of inner alchemy, allowing the flames of his consciousness to illuminate his path.

The Fourth Portal: The Portal of Water
The Portal of Water represents fluidity, emotions, and the depths of our subconscious. It is through this portal that we connect with our intuitive nature, the wellspring of wisdom that lies within. Practices associated with the Fourth Portal include working with water as a purifying element, engaging in reflective practices, and cultivating emotional awareness.

Practical Example: Let us envision Pema, a sensitive practitioner, performing a ritual of water scrying. Pema fills a bowl with pure water and gazes into its reflective surface, allowing her mind to quiet and her intuition to awaken. As she observes the ripples and patterns forming in the water, Pema attunes herself to the messages that arise from her subconscious mind. Through the exploration of the Fourth Portal, Pema deepens her connection with her emotional landscape and taps into the intuitive guidance that flows from within.

As we journey through the Four Portals, we awaken to the interconnectedness of our being with the divine realms. By engaging in practices that honor these portals, we gain access to profound wisdom, expanded consciousness, and transformative experiences. In the next chapter, we will explore the realm of siddhis, extraordinary powers that transcend the limits of the physical world. Join me as we uncover the secrets to attaining these remarkable abilities and understanding their spiritual significance.

CHAPTER 8: SIDDHIS: ATTAINING EXTRAORDINARY POWERS

Within the realm of Tibetan magic, there exists a profound pursuit of extraordinary powers known as siddhis. These siddhis transcend the boundaries of the physical world and allow practitioners to tap into the vast reservoir of their inherent potential. In this chapter, we will embark on a journey into the realm of siddhis, exploring the elaborate magical rites and practices that enable the attainment of these extraordinary abilities.

The path to obtaining siddhis requires unwavering dedication, discipline, and a deep understanding of the subtle energies that pervade the universe. By harnessing these energies and aligning oneself with the forces of nature, practitioners can awaken dormant faculties within themselves and manifest incredible powers. It is important to note that the pursuit of siddhis should be approached with humility, reverence, and a genuine intention to benefit all beings.

One of the foundational practices for attaining siddhis is the cultivation of focused concentration. Through rigorous training of the mind, practitioners learn to quiet the mental chatter and enter states of deep meditative absorption. In these states, the mind becomes clear, focused, and receptive to the subtle vibrations of the universe. With such refined concentration, practitioners can begin to explore the vast realms of possibility and access the wellspring of their latent abilities.

Practical Example: Imagine a dedicated practitioner named Sonam engaging in the practice of samatha meditation, the cultivation of tranquil abiding. Sonam finds a secluded spot amidst the breathtaking beauty of the Himalayan mountains, assuming a comfortable posture. With each breath, he allows his mind to settle and his awareness to rest on a chosen object of meditation, such as a flickering candle flame. As Sonam persists in his practice, he gradually enters deeper states of concentration, transcending ordinary perceptions and tapping into the boundless potential within himself. Through his unwavering dedication to samatha meditation, Sonam awakens the seeds of extraordinary powers within his being.

Another vital aspect of the journey towards siddhis is the understanding and manipulation of subtle energies. Tibetan magical traditions emphasize the existence of channels, or nadis, through which prana, the life force, flows. By purifying and harmonizing these energy channels, practitioners can enhance the flow of prana and awaken dormant abilities.

Practical Example: Let us envision a practitioner named Tenzin engaging in the practice of Kundalini yoga, a powerful system for awakening the dormant energy coiled at the base of the spine. Tenzin assumes an asana, or physical posture, that facilitates the movement of prana through the central channel of the body. Through focused breathwork, visualization, and mantra recitation, Tenzin directs the awakened Kundalini energy upwards, piercing through each chakra and unlocking the corresponding siddhis associated with each energetic center. By skillfully manipulating the subtle energies within his being, Tenzin opens the door to extraordinary abilities and experiences.

It is crucial to approach the pursuit of siddhis with humility and a genuine commitment to the welfare of all beings. The acquisition of these extraordinary powers should never be pursued for selfish gain or egoic gratification. Instead, the cultivation of siddhis should be guided by compassion, wisdom, and a deep desire to contribute to the betterment of the world.

In the next part of our journey, we will explore the darker realms of Tibetan magic as we delve into Bonpa Shamanism, a mystical practice steeped in history and the understanding of necromantic arts. Join me as we unravel the ancient wisdom and explore the profound mysteries of this esoteric tradition.

CHAPTER 9: BONPA SHAMANISM: THE NECROMANTIC ART

Within the vast tapestry of Tibetan magical traditions, an ancient and enigmatic path known as Bonpa Shamanism weaves its way through the realm of spirituality. Delving into the depths of this esoteric practice, we uncover the intricate rituals, necromantic arts, and profound historical significance that define Bonpa Shamanism. In this chapter, we will explore the mystique of this dark and ancient world, shedding light on its hidden wisdom and the transformative power it holds.

Bonpa Shamanism represents a unique facet of Tibetan magical practices, rooted in a deep connection to the natural world and the forces that shape it. This tradition, steeped in antiquity, has endured the passage of time, carrying with it a rich tapestry of ceremonies, invocations, and shamanic techniques that bridge the realms of the living and the dead.

Practitioners of Bonpa Shamanism navigate the liminal spaces between the physical and spiritual dimensions, channeling the energies of the unseen and invoking ancestral spirits. Through intricate rituals and the guidance of an experienced shaman, one gains access to the wisdom and powers of these otherworldly beings, fostering healing, protection, and guidance.

Practical Example: Imagine a Bonpa Shaman named Lhakpa, adorned in ceremonial robes and donning sacred adornments, performing a ritual to commune with the spirits of departed ancestors. Lhakpa creates an altar adorned with offerings, including bowls of water, incense, and food. With steady hands, Lhakpa beats a sacred drum and chants ancient incantations, calling forth the spirits to partake in the ceremony. As the rhythm of the drum intensifies, Lhakpa enters a trance-like state, becoming a conduit between the realms. Through this powerful connection, Lhakpa seeks guidance, wisdom, and healing for the community.

While the practices of Bonpa Shamanism may seem mysterious and alluring, it is essential to approach them with respect, reverence, and a deep understanding of the profound responsibility that comes with engaging in necromantic arts. The practitioner must develop a strong connection with the natural elements, maintain purity of intention, and cultivate unwavering compassion for all beings.

Bonpa Shamanism offers a pathway to explore the depths of the human psyche, confront inner shadows, and navigate the complex web of life and death. By engaging with the necromantic arts, practitioners gain insight into the mysteries of existence, embracing the cyclical nature of birth, death, and rebirth.

In the next chapter, we will delve into the realm of thought forms, unveiling the techniques of mental visualization exercises to manifest the mind's creations. Join me as we explore the potential and purpose of these ethereal entities known as tulpas and their profound impact on our spiritual journey.

CHAPTER 10: THOUGHT FORMS: MANIFESTING THE MIND'S CREATIONS

In the realm of Tibetan magic, the power of the mind takes center stage as we explore the fascinating concept of thought forms. These ethereal entities, known as tulpas, are manifestations of the mind's creative potential, shaped and given life through the focused power of intention and visualization. In this chapter, we will delve into the art of creating thought forms, understanding their purpose, and exploring their vast potential within the realm of Tibetan magical practices.

Thought forms are the product of the mind's ability to shape energy and consciousness. They are visualized entities imbued with specific qualities and intentions. As practitioners of Tibetan magic, we have the capacity to bring these thought forms to life, infusing them with energy and purpose.

The creation of a thought form begins with a clear intention. One must envision the desired qualities, attributes, or outcomes that the thought form is intended to embody. Through focused visualization, we mold and shape the energetic essence, giving it form and substance within the subtle realms.

Practical Example: Let's imagine a practitioner named Dawa who seeks to create a thought form to enhance their concentration and focus during meditation. Dawa finds a quiet space, enters a meditative state, and visualizes a radiant sphere of light before them. With every breath, the sphere grows brighter and more vibrant, pulsating with focused energy. Dawa imbues the sphere with qualities of unwavering concentration, tranquility, and clarity of mind. As the visualization intensifies, the thought form gains strength and presence, ready to assist Dawa in their meditation practice.

Thought forms, once created, possess a degree of autonomy within the energetic realms. They can interact with the practitioner and the external environment, serving as guides, protectors, or catalysts for transformation. However, it is crucial to maintain a sense of control and clarity over the thought form's purpose and boundaries to avoid unintended consequences.

While thought forms can be powerful allies on the spiritual path, they also require responsible practice. It is essential to monitor their development, ensure their alignment with one's intentions, and dissolve them when their purpose has been fulfilled. Neglecting this duty may allow thought forms to become unruly or inadvertently influence the practitioner's mental and emotional state.

CHAPTER 11: VISIONS: GLIMPSES INTO HIGHER REALMS

In the realm of Tibetan magic, visions hold a significant place. They are glimpses into higher realms, windows into the vast tapestry of consciousness that extends beyond our mundane reality. Visions offer us profound insights, spiritual growth, and personal transformation. In this chapter, we will delve into the phenomenon of visions and explore their role in expanding our understanding of the enchanted Himalayas.

Visions are not mere flights of fancy or random hallucinations. They are sacred encounters, invitations from the divine to explore the limitless possibilities of existence. Through visions, we can gain access to hidden knowledge, receive guidance from spiritual beings, and even catch glimpses of our true selves.

One way to experience visions is through deep meditation. By quieting the mind and focusing our awareness inward, we create the space for extraordinary encounters. In this state, the boundaries between the physical and spiritual realms blur, and we become receptive to the messages and visions that arise.

Practical Example:

Find a peaceful and quiet place where you can sit comfortably. Close your eyes and take a few deep breaths, allowing your body and mind to relax. Bring your attention to the present moment, letting go of any thoughts or concerns.

Now, imagine yourself surrounded by a sphere of pure white light, a protective cocoon of divine energy. Feel its warmth and unconditional love enveloping you, creating a safe space for exploration.

As you continue to breathe deeply, envision a serene and

beautiful landscape unfolding before you. It may be a meadow, a mountaintop, or a tranquil lake. Allow the details to materialize in your mind's eye.

In this serene setting, call upon a guide or deity whose wisdom you seek. It could be Avalokiteshvara, Manjushri, or any other deity that resonates with you. Invoke their presence and ask for their guidance and blessings on your journey.

Stay present and open to whatever arises. You may witness vivid images, symbols, or scenes unfolding in your mind. Observe them without judgment or attachment, allowing them to come and go naturally.

When your meditation comes to a close, take a few moments to reflect on your experience. What insights did you gain? What emotions or sensations did you encounter? Journaling about your visions can help deepen your understanding and provide a record of your spiritual growth.

Remember, visions can be subtle or profound, and their meanings may not always be immediately clear. Trust in the process and be patient with yourself. With time and practice, your ability to access higher realms through visions will expand, and the insights you receive will become more profound.

By engaging with visions, we open ourselves to the interconnectedness of all things. We glimpse the vastness of the universe within our own consciousness. These experiences inspire us to seek truth, to cultivate compassion, and to embrace the magical journey that lies before us.

In the next chapter, we will explore the transformative practice of physical yoga and its profound role in harmonizing the body, mind, and spirit. Through the union of these elements, we unlock our true potential and continue our quest for self-mastery.

Remember, the enchanted Himalayas have much to offer, and as we venture deeper into this mystical land, we uncover hidden treasures that can shape our lives and illuminate our paths.

CHAPTER 12: PHYSICAL YOGA: THE UNION OF BODY AND SPIRIT

Within the vast tapestry of Tibetan magical practices, physical yoga occupies a profound place. It is a transformative discipline that harmonizes the body, mind, and spirit, facilitating a deeper connection with the mystical energies of the enchanted Himalayas. In this chapter, we will explore the ancient and profound practice of physical yoga and its role in unlocking our true potential.

Physical yoga is not merely a series of physical postures; it is a sacred path of self-discovery and self-mastery. Through deliberate movements, breath control, and focused awareness, we unite our physical being with our spiritual essence. This union allows us to tap into the limitless power within us and cultivate a heightened state of consciousness.

Practical Example:

Begin by finding a quiet space where you can dedicate time to your physical yoga practice. Wear loose and comfortable clothing that allows for unrestricted movement. Take a moment to set an intention for your practice, whether it is to cultivate inner peace, strengthen your connection with the divine, or enhance your physical well-being.

Start with a gentle warm-up to prepare your body for the deeper practice ahead. Engage in gentle stretches, loosening your muscles and joints. Pay attention to your breath, inhaling deeply through your nose and exhaling fully through your mouth.

Now, move into a series of asanas, or physical postures, focusing on synchronizing your breath with each movement. Begin with simple poses such as Mountain Pose (Tadasana), forward folds, or gentle twists. As you progress, you can explore more complex postures like Warrior Pose (Virabhadrasana) or Tree Pose (Vrikshasana).

Remember to maintain a steady and conscious breath throughout your practice. Let your breath guide you as you flow from one pose to another, remaining fully present in the sensations of your body and the movements of your breath. Allow any thoughts or distractions to drift away, focusing your attention solely on the practice at hand.

As you hold each pose, explore your inner landscape. Observe any physical sensations, emotions, or energetic shifts that arise. Notice how the asanas affect your body and mind, fostering a sense of balance, strength, and peace.

Conclude your practice with a period of relaxation and reflection. Lie down in Savasana, the Corpse Pose, and surrender your body and mind to complete stillness. Allow yourself to absorb the benefits of your practice and bask in the sense of unity between your physical and spiritual self.

Physical yoga is not confined to the mat; it is a way of life. By integrating the principles of yoga into your daily routine, you can infuse magic into every aspect of your existence. Carry the awareness and mindfulness cultivated on the mat into your interactions with others, your work, and your connection with nature. These techniques offer profound insights into the untapped potential of the human body and provide a gateway to extraordinary experiences.

Remember, the practice of physical yoga is a gateway to self-discovery, an invitation to unlock your hidden potential, and a means to align your body, mind, and spirit with the mystical energies of the Himalayas.

CHAPTER 13: THE INNER FIRE: UNLOCKING THE BODY'S HEAT MECHANISM

Within the mystical realm of Tibetan magic lies a profound understanding of the body's untapped potential. It is believed that within each of us resides a sacred fire, an inner flame that can be harnessed and controlled. In this chapter, we will embark on a journey to discover the ancient techniques of unlocking the body's heat mechanism, offering profound insights into the vast potential of the human body.

The Inner Fire is a powerful force that resides within our core, fueling our vitality and connecting us to the energies of the universe. By cultivating and controlling this fiery energy, we can awaken dormant powers, heighten our consciousness, and achieve extraordinary feats. Through dedicated practice and disciplined focus, we can kindle the flames of the Inner Fire, propelling us towards the realms of transcendence.

Practical Example:

Begin by finding a quiet and secluded space where you can comfortably sit or lie down. Take a few moments to settle into a relaxed and focused state. Close your eyes and bring your attention to your breath, allowing it to become slow, deep, and steady.

As you inhale, visualize a radiant ball of golden light entering your body, traveling down to your abdomen. As you exhale, imagine this golden light expanding and spreading throughout your entire body, bringing warmth and vitality to every cell. Visualize the flames of the Inner Fire growing brighter and more intense with each breath.

Now, shift your awareness to your navel area, known as the lower dantian. Visualize a small flame residing within this sacred space.

As you inhale, imagine your breath fueling this flame, making it grow larger and brighter. As you exhale, feel the warmth and energy of the Inner Fire radiating throughout your entire body.

With each breath, deepen your connection to the Inner Fire. Visualize it spreading beyond your physical body, expanding into your energetic field, and extending to the farthest reaches of the universe. Feel the power and potential of this sacred fire, knowing that it connects you to the divine energies that flow through all things.

As you continue this practice, you may experience sensations of warmth, tingling, or an intensified sense of energy. Embrace these sensations and allow them to guide you deeper into the realm of the Inner Fire. Explore variations of breath control, such as retention or elongation of the breath, to further refine your connection and control over this powerful energy.

Remember, the practice of unlocking the body's heat mechanism requires patience, dedication, and respect for your body's limitations. Start with shorter practice sessions and gradually increase the duration as your capacity develops. Be mindful of any physical or energetic sensations that arise and adjust your practice accordingly.

By unlocking the Inner Fire, we tap into a wellspring of vitality, heightened consciousness, and spiritual transformation. Through diligent practice, we can harness this ancient wisdom to fuel our magical endeavors and navigate the enchanting Himalayas with grace and power.

Remember, the Inner Fire is not separate from us—it is a part of our essence. Embrace its radiance, nurture its flame, and let its transformative power guide you on your path of self-discovery.

CHAPTER 14: BREATH AS A GATEWAY TO THE DIVINE

In the realm of Tibetan magic, the breath holds immense power and serves as a profound gateway to the divine. Our breath is not only a vital physiological function but also a sacred tool that can be consciously harnessed to deepen our spiritual practice, expand our consciousness, and connect with the vast realms of the unseen.

Breathing exercises have been revered in Tibetan culture for centuries as a means to purify the mind, harmonize the body, and awaken dormant spiritual potentials. By bringing conscious awareness to our breath and employing specific techniques, we can tap into the transformative power that lies within us.

Practical Example:

Find a peaceful and serene space where you can sit comfortably, with your spine straight and your body relaxed. Gently close your eyes and turn your attention inward. Begin by taking a few deep breaths, inhaling slowly and deeply through your nose, allowing your abdomen to expand fully. Exhale slowly and completely, feeling the release of any tension or stress.

As you settle into a rhythm, shift your focus to the natural flow of your breath. Notice the coolness of the air as you inhale and the warmth as you exhale. Observe the rise and fall of your chest and the gentle expansion and contraction of your abdomen.

Now, bring your awareness to the present moment, to the here and now. With each inhalation, imagine that you are drawing in pure, vibrant energy from the universe, filling your entire being with revitalizing light. Feel this energy permeating every cell of your body, awakening and nourishing your spirit.

As you exhale, envision releasing any stagnant or negative energy, allowing it to dissolve and transform into pure light. Feel yourself becoming lighter, more open, and more attuned to the subtle energies of the divine.

To deepen your practice, explore different breathing techniques. One powerful method is the "Fourfold Breath." Inhale deeply for a count of four, hold the breath for a count of four, exhale slowly for a count of four, and hold the breath out for a count of four. Repeat this cycle several times, allowing each breath to become more soothing and profound.

Another technique is "Alternate Nostril Breathing." Gently close your right nostril with your right thumb and inhale deeply through your left nostril. Then, close your left nostril with your ring finger and release your right nostril, exhaling fully. Inhale again through the right nostril, close it, and exhale through the left. Continue this pattern, focusing on the balance and harmony created by the alternating breath.

Through regular practice of conscious breathing, you can cultivate a deep sense of presence, clarity, and connection with the divine. The breath becomes a guiding force, leading you to the profound depths of your being and beyond.

As you explore the transformative power of breath, be gentle with yourself and honor your body's natural rhythm. Allow the breath to guide you, listening to its subtle whispers of wisdom and insight. Embrace the sacredness of each breath, for within it lies the essence of life itself.

Remember, the breath is a precious gift that can serve as your compass on the path of spiritual awakening. Breathe consciously, breathe deeply, and breathe in the divine.

CHAPTER 15: MESSAGES ON THE WIND: COMMUNICATING BEYOND BOUNDARIES

In the enchanted realm of Tibetan magic, the power of communication extends far beyond the constraints of physical words. As practitioners, we can tap into the mystical art of sending messages on the wind, connecting with higher realms and transcending the limitations of space and time. Through this ancient practice, we open ourselves to profound wisdom and guidance, fostering a deep connection with the unseen forces that surround us.

The wind, with its invisible currents and ever-changing nature, serves as a conduit for communication between realms. By harnessing its power, we can convey our intentions, prayers, and messages to the divine and receive responses in subtle and unexpected ways.

Practical Example:

Begin by finding a quiet and serene spot in nature, where you can feel a gentle breeze upon your skin. Stand with your feet firmly planted on the ground, grounding yourself and opening your heart to the vastness of the universe.

Take a moment to quiet your mind and bring your awareness to the present moment. Feel the sensation of the wind as it caresses your face, acknowledging its presence and power.

Now, visualize your intention or message as a radiant ball of light within your heart center. See it growing brighter and more vibrant with each breath.

As you exhale, imagine that this ball of light expands outward, merging with the surrounding air. Feel the energy of your message infusing the wind, carrying your intentions and desires to the unseen realms.

With a focused mind, speak your message silently or aloud, allowing the words to merge with the wind and become one with the elements. Trust that the wind will carry your message to its intended destination.

Stay open and receptive, for the response may come in various forms—a sudden gust of wind, a whisper in the leaves, or a subtle shift in the environment. Be attentive to signs and synchronicities, as the wind has a way of weaving its magic through the tapestry of our lives.

Remember that communication on the wind is not limited to sending messages. It is also a profound practice of listening and receiving. As you stand in the presence of the wind, open your heart and mind to the subtle whispers of the universe. Be receptive to the guidance and wisdom that may be conveyed through the rustling of leaves or the soft caress of the breeze.

Through the art of communicating on the wind, we transcend the limitations of the physical realm and enter into a realm of interconnectedness and unity. We realize that we are part of something greater, and our voices can be heard beyond the boundaries of our immediate surroundings.

May the winds carry your messages and intentions to the sacred realms, and may the responses you receive fill your heart with divine guidance.

CHAPTER 16: TARA: THE COMPASSIONATE GODDESS

In the vast tapestry of Tibetan deities, one figure stands out for her boundless compassion and unwavering dedication to alleviating suffering—the divine goddess Tara. Known as the Mother of all Buddhas, Tara embodies the essence of enlightened femininity and serves as a beacon of love, wisdom, and grace in the realm of Tibetan magic. In this chapter, we immerse ourselves in the captivating realm of Tara, gaining an understanding of her significance in Tibetan culture and exploring practices that allow us to connect with her profound wisdom and compassionate energy.

Unveiling the Essence of Tara

To truly appreciate the divine presence of Tara, we must delve into her origins and the symbolism she embodies. Tara, whose name translates to "star" or "savior," is believed to have emerged from the compassionate tears of Avalokiteshvara, the Bodhisattva of Compassion. As such, Tara represents the nurturing and protective aspects of femininity, offering solace and guidance to those who seek her aid.

Tara's divine nature is often depicted in various forms, each carrying its own unique attributes and symbolism. The most common forms are Green Tara and White Tara. Green Tara, with her emerald hue, embodies active compassion and swift action. She is revered for her ability to swiftly respond to the cries of sentient beings and protect them from harm. On the other hand, White Tara radiates serenity and tranquility, embodying the healing power of compassion and offering blessings of longevity and spiritual nourishment.

Connecting with Tara's Wisdom and Grace

The magical practices associated with Tara are diverse, ranging from simple devotional rituals to complex visualizations. Here, we explore a few practices that can help us forge a profound connection with Tara's wisdom and grace.

Invocation and Mantra Recitation: Begin your practice by creating a sacred space, adorned with images or statues of Tara. Close your eyes, center yourself, and visualize Tara's radiant presence before you. With sincerity and devotion, recite her mantra: "Om Tare Tuttare Ture Soha." Allow the sound and vibrations of the mantra to resonate within you, invoking Tara's compassionate energy and opening the channels for her guidance.

Visualization and Offering: Visualize yourself surrounded by a luminous emerald light, symbolizing Tara's compassionate energy enveloping you. As you bask in her radiance, offer her the purest intentions of your heart. Imagine presenting her with symbolic offerings, such as flowers, incense, or offerings of your own creation. With each offering, cultivate a sense of gratitude for her presence and an open heart to receive her blessings.

Meditation on Compassion: Find a quiet space where you can sit comfortably and undisturbed. Close your eyes and focus on your breath, allowing your mind to settle. Gradually shift your attention to the seed of compassion within you, nurturing it with each inhale and exhale. Visualize Tara beside you, her compassionate gaze affirming and amplifying your own compassionate nature. Breathe in the essence of her compassion, allowing it to infuse your being. Rest in this state of profound empathy, knowing that Tara's grace supports your journey towards greater compassion for yourself and others.

Practical Examples of Tara's Guidance

Tara's compassionate energy extends beyond the confines of meditation and ritual; it permeates our daily lives, guiding us through challenges and nurturing our growth. Here are a few practical examples of how we can invoke Tara's presence in our daily experiences:

Compassionate Listening: In your interactions with others, strive to cultivate compassionate listening. Take a moment to set aside your own judgments and preconceptions, and truly hear the needs and concerns of those around you. Approach conversations with an open heart and a genuine desire to understand, offering support and solace, much like Tara would extend her compassionate ear.

Acts of Kindness: Let Tara's compassion inspire you to perform acts of kindness and generosity. Engage in small gestures of compassion, such as volunteering your time for a cause you believe in, helping a stranger in need, or simply offering a kind word or smile to brighten someone's day. These acts ripple outwards, spreading the seeds of compassion and creating positive change.

Self-Compassion and Inner Healing: Tara's grace reminds us to extend compassion to ourselves as well. Take time to nurture your own well-being through self-care practices, such as meditation, journaling, or engaging in activities that bring you joy. Treat yourself with the same gentleness and love that Tara extends to all beings, recognizing your own intrinsic worth and embracing your journey of self-discovery and healing.

By embracing the teachings and practices associated with Tara, we open ourselves to the transformative power of compassion. Through invoking her wisdom and grace, we not only deepen our connection with Tibetan magical traditions but also embark on a path of personal growth, healing, and service to others. In the next chapter, we reflect on the transformative journey through the secrets of Himalayan magic, offering insights and personal reflections that will illuminate your own path.

CHAPTER 17: THE PATH UNVEILED:
REFLECTIONS AND INSIGHTS

As we come to the penultimate chapter of our journey through the enchanted Himalayas, it is time to pause and reflect upon the profound insights and transformative experiences we have encountered. The secrets of Tibetan magic have illuminated our path, revealing the hidden potential within ourselves and the interconnectedness of all things. In this chapter, we delve into the reflections and personal insights that have emerged from our exploration of Himalayan magic, guiding us towards a deeper understanding of ourselves and the world around us.

Embracing the Inner Alchemy

Throughout our exploration of Tibetan magical practices, a consistent theme has emerged—the power of harnessing our inner energies. From the ancient technique of Tumo, which ignites the inner fire, to the practice of Dream Yoga, which awakens the subconscious, we have witnessed the transformative potential that lies within us. These practices have taught us that true magic begins by delving deep within ourselves, by nurturing our connection to the vast reservoir of energy and wisdom that resides within.

Practical Example: One practical way to embrace the inner alchemy is through a daily meditation practice. Set aside a dedicated time each day to sit in stillness and silence. As you close your eyes and turn your attention inward, observe the sensations in your body, the thoughts passing through your mind, and the emotions that arise. By simply witnessing these aspects of your being without judgment or attachment, you begin to cultivate a deeper awareness of your inner landscape and connect with the wellspring of inner wisdom that is always available to you.

Surrendering to the Flow of the Universe

Tibetan magical practices remind us of the importance of surrendering to the flow of the universe, rather than clinging to control and resistance. We have explored the power of sound, rhythm, and chanting, which allow us to align ourselves with the harmonious vibrations of the cosmos. By surrendering to the natural rhythms and cycles of life, we open ourselves to the limitless possibilities that exist beyond our limited perceptions.

Practical Example: Engaging in a nature-based practice can help us surrender to the flow of the universe. Take a walk in a natural setting and immerse yourself in the sights, sounds, and sensations of the environment. Allow yourself to be fully present, observing the interconnectedness of all living beings and the intricate dance of nature. As you do so, let go of any expectations or desires and simply surrender to the beauty and wisdom that surrounds you.

Cultivating Gratitude and Compassion

Gratitude and compassion are essential qualities that permeate the tapestry of Tibetan magical practices. We have witnessed the compassionate nature of Tara and explored the power of compassion in our daily lives. Gratitude opens our hearts to the abundance and beauty of life, while compassion allows us to extend a helping hand to those in need, fostering interconnectedness and healing.

Practical Example: Create a gratitude journal where you can regularly write down three things you are grateful for each day. Cultivate a sense of appreciation for the small blessings in your life, such as a warm cup of tea or a kind gesture from a friend. Additionally, find ways to extend compassion to others, whether it's through volunteering, acts of kindness, or simply offering a listening ear to someone who is in need.

Trusting the Unseen Forces

Tibetan magical practices invite us to trust in the unseen forces that shape our reality. From the exploration of visions and higher realms to the communication through messages on the wind, we have witnessed the presence of these subtle energies that guide and support us on our journey. By trusting in these unseen forces, we can tap into a wellspring of inspiration and guidance that transcends our limited understanding.

Practical Example: Engage in a daily ritual of connecting with the unseen forces. Find a quiet space where you can sit in solitude and silence. Close your eyes and visualize yourself surrounded by a sphere of divine light. Surrender any doubts or fears and trust that you are being held and guided by benevolent forces. Open your heart to receive any messages, insights, or guidance that may arise, trusting that you are supported on your path.

Integration and Continued Exploration

As we reflect on our journey through the secrets of Himalayan magic, it is crucial to recognize that this is not the end but rather a new beginning. The insights and practices we have explored are not meant to be compartmentalized but rather integrated into our daily lives. We are encouraged to continue our exploration, to deepen our understanding, and to embrace our own unique magical path.

Practical Example: Identify one Tibetan magical practice that resonates deeply with you and commit to integrating it into your daily life. Whether it is a breathing exercise, a visualization technique, or a mantra, dedicate yourself to practicing it consistently. Observe how this practice enhances your well-being, deepens your connection to the divine, and enriches your overall experience of life.

As we conclude our reflections and insights, we stand on the threshold of a new phase in our magical journey—the integration of these teachings into our daily lives. In the final chapter, we will explore practical suggestions for incorporating magical practices into everyday life, fostering personal growth, and spiritual development. The enchantment of the Himalayas awaits us as we embrace the never-ending quest for wisdom, transformation, and connection with the divine.

CHAPTER 18: INTEGRATING
MAGIC INTO DAILY LIFE

As we have journeyed through the depths of Tibetan magical practices, we have discovered profound insights and transformative experiences. The secrets of the enchanted Himalayas have not only opened our minds to new possibilities but also provided us with practical tools to incorporate magic into our daily lives. In this chapter, we explore how to infuse the essence of Tibetan magic into our routines and interactions, fostering personal growth and spiritual development.

Creating Sacred Spaces

One powerful way to integrate magic into our daily lives is by creating sacred spaces within our living environments. These spaces serve as portals to the spiritual realm, providing a refuge for meditation, reflection, and the practice of magical rituals. By consecrating a corner of our homes or even a small altar, we invite the energies of the divine into our everyday existence.

Practical Example: Find a quiet and secluded area in your home where you can create a sacred space. Clear the area of clutter and place objects that hold personal meaning to you, such as crystals, candles, or sacred symbols. This space will serve as a reminder of the sacred in the midst of the mundane, allowing you to connect with the subtle energies and find solace in your daily practice.

Ritualizing Everyday Actions

Every action we take has the potential to be infused with intention and magic. By ritualizing our everyday actions, we bring mindfulness and purpose into the simplest tasks, turning them into transformative experiences. From preparing and consuming meals to cleansing and self-care routines, each act becomes an opportunity for connection, gratitude, and personal empowerment.

Practical Example: Before you start your day, create a morning ritual that sets a positive and magical tone for the hours ahead. This could involve lighting a candle, reciting an affirmation, or performing a short visualization exercise. As you go about your morning routine, infuse each action with intention and awareness, such as mindfully brushing your teeth, savoring your breakfast, or expressing gratitude for the new day.

Connecting with the Natural World

The natural world is a wellspring of magic and wisdom, and by forging a deeper connection with nature, we can enhance our own magical journey. Take time to immerse yourself in the beauty of the outdoors, whether it's a walk in the park, tending to a garden, or simply observing the cycles of the moon. By aligning ourselves with the rhythms of nature, we tap into a reservoir of inspiration, healing, and spiritual growth.

Practical Example: Dedicate regular moments to connect with nature, even if you live in an urban environment. Step outside during your lunch break and find a quiet spot where you can sit and observe the surrounding trees, flowers, or sky. Take a few deep breaths, grounding yourself in the present moment, and invite the energy of the natural world to flow through you. As you do so, feel a sense of oneness with the earth and allow its magic to permeate your being.

Cultivating Mindfulness and Awareness

One of the fundamental principles of Tibetan magical practices is cultivating mindfulness and awareness in every aspect of our lives. By being fully present in each moment, we heighten our sensitivity to the subtle energies, synchronicities, and opportunities for growth that surround us. Through mindfulness, we awaken to the magic that exists in the here and now.

Practical Example: Incorporate mindfulness practices into your daily routine, such as mindfulness meditation or mindful walking. Choose a specific activity, such as washing the dishes or taking a shower, and bring your complete attention to it. Notice the sensory details, the movements of your body, and the thoughts and emotions that arise. By engaging with these activities mindfully, you cultivate a deep sense of presence and open yourself to the magic that lies within them.

As we conclude this chapter on integrating magic into daily life, we realize that the essence of Tibetan magical practices extends far beyond specific rituals or techniques. It permeates our existence, inviting us to embrace a magical perspective in every moment. By creating sacred spaces, ritualizing everyday actions, connecting with nature, and cultivating mindfulness, we infuse our lives with wonder, purpose, and spiritual growth. The magical journey continues as we honor the sacred and embark on the never-ending quest for wisdom, transformation, and connection with the divine.

CHAPTER 19: HONORING THE SACRED: RESPECTING TIBETAN CULTURE AND TRADITIONS

Throughout our exploration of Tibetan magical practices, we have been granted a glimpse into a sacred tradition that spans centuries. As we embark on this final chapter, it is vital to acknowledge and honor the rich tapestry of Tibetan culture and traditions from which these magical teachings arise. By embracing respect, reverence, and deep gratitude for this sacred knowledge, we ensure the preservation and continuity of this profound heritage.

Cultivating Cultural Awareness

To truly honor Tibetan culture and traditions, it is essential to cultivate a genuine understanding and appreciation of its values, customs, and beliefs. By immersing ourselves in the essence of Tibetan culture, we develop a sensitivity and respect for the interconnectedness of spirituality, daily life, and the natural world.

Practical Example: Take the time to explore Tibetan art, literature, and music. Engage in conversations with Tibetan individuals or scholars knowledgeable about Tibetan culture. Attend cultural events or festivals that celebrate Tibetan traditions. By actively seeking out these experiences, we deepen our understanding of the culture and forge a connection to its roots.

Respecting Rituals and Ceremonies

Tibetan culture is replete with sacred rituals and ceremonies that are an integral part of everyday life. These rituals serve as vehicles for spiritual connection, healing, and the preservation of wisdom. To honor Tibetan culture, we must approach these rituals with reverence and respect, recognizing their significance and participating with sincerity.

Practical Example: If you are invited to witness or participate in a Tibetan ritual or ceremony, approach it with an open heart and mind. Familiarize yourself with the proper etiquette and protocols, observing the behaviors and actions of those around you. Be mindful of your presence and avoid any disruptive or disrespectful behavior. By engaging in these rituals with humility and attentiveness, we honor the sacred intentions they hold.

Supporting Tibetan Communities

One powerful way to honor Tibetan culture and traditions is by supporting Tibetan communities and organizations. By offering our assistance, solidarity, and respect, we contribute to the preservation and continuity of Tibetan heritage. This can be done through various means, such as supporting local Tibetan businesses, engaging in cultural exchange programs, or advocating for Tibetan rights and freedoms.

Practical Example: Seek out Tibetan-owned businesses and artisans when purchasing Tibetan crafts, artwork, or products. Attend events organized by Tibetan communities and support their initiatives. Educate yourself and others about the challenges faced by Tibetans and lend your voice to their causes. By actively supporting Tibetan communities, we become agents of change and contribute to the flourishing of Tibetan culture.

Preserving and Sharing the Knowledge

The sacred knowledge and wisdom contained within Tibetan magical practices are a precious gift passed down through generations. To honor this legacy, we must play our part in preserving and sharing this knowledge responsibly and authentically. By recognizing the importance of lineage, respecting the teachings, and safeguarding their integrity, we become stewards of the sacred traditions.

Practical Example: If you choose to share the magical practices you have learned, do so with utmost care and reverence. Acknowledge and credit the sources of your knowledge, honoring the lineage from which it has come. Avoid distorting or appropriating the teachings, ensuring their authenticity and integrity are maintained. By upholding the values and principles of the Tibetan tradition, we ensure the perpetuation of this sacred knowledge.

In honoring the sacred, we acknowledge the interconnectedness of all beings and the wisdom embedded within Tibetan culture and traditions. By cultivating cultural awareness, respecting rituals and ceremonies, supporting Tibetan communities, and preserving and sharing the knowledge, we ensure that the essence of Tibetan magic continues to thrive and inspire generations to come. As we conclude this chapter, let us carry the torch of reverence and gratitude, knowing that through our actions, we contribute to the preservation and celebration of the enchanting heritage of the Tibetan people.

CHAPTER 20: THE NEVER-ENDING QUEST: CONTINUING THE MAGICAL JOURNEY

As we reach the final chapter of "Tibetan Magic: The Enchanted Himalayas," we find ourselves at the precipice of a new beginning rather than an end. The mystical journey through the realms of Tibetan magic has only just begun to unveil the vast tapestry of possibilities that await those who dare to explore. In this chapter, we will embark on a quest to further nourish our magical spirits, offering insights, resources, and guidance for the continuation of our enchanted journey.

Embracing Personal Exploration

Just as each individual is unique, so too is their path in the realm of magic. It is crucial to embrace your personal journey of exploration, honoring your own instincts and intuition. There are countless avenues to be pursued and boundless knowledge to be gained. Trust in your inner wisdom as you navigate the uncharted territories of the magical arts.

Cultivating Curiosity

A curious mind is a fertile ground for magical growth. Allow yourself to be captivated by the mysteries that surround you. Seek out new perspectives, delve into different magical traditions, and expand your understanding of the world. Remember that the thirst for knowledge and the pursuit of wisdom are lifelong companions on this never-ending quest.

Building a Magical Library

A treasure trove of knowledge awaits within the pages of books. Create your own magical library, filled with works of ancient wisdom and contemporary insights. Seek out texts on various magical traditions, mythology, esoteric practices, and spiritual philosophy. Let the words of sages and mystics from different eras and cultures be your guide, sparking inspiration and deepening your understanding of the magical arts.

Practical Example: Consider adding the following books to your magical library:

"The Secret Teachings of Padmasambhava" by Jigme Lingpa
"The Golden Bough" by James George Frazer
"The Kybalion" by The Three Initiates
"The Way of Wyrd" by Brian Bates
"The Art and Practice of Astral Projection" by Ophiel

Seeking Wisdom from Teachers and Mentors
In any pursuit, the guidance of experienced mentors can greatly enrich the learning process. Seek out teachers who embody the principles and practices you resonate with. Engage in respectful dialogue, attend workshops and seminars, and participate in magical communities where knowledge is shared and experiences are celebrated. Remember, the bonds we forge with wise individuals can illuminate our path and accelerate our growth.

The Power of Self-Reflection
Throughout your magical journey, take the time to reflect on your experiences and insights. Self-reflection allows you to integrate newfound wisdom into your being, nurturing personal growth and deepening your connection to the magical realms. Journaling, meditation, and contemplation are invaluable tools in this ongoing process of self-discovery and understanding.

Practical Example: Set aside a few moments each day to reflect on your magical practices. Consider questions such as: What have I learned? How have I grown? What challenges have I encountered? What successes have I celebrated? Embrace the transformative power of self-reflection.

Connecting with a Magical Community
Magic is a tapestry woven by countless souls across time and space. Seek out fellow travelers who share your passion for the magical arts. Engage in discussions, share experiences, and learn

from one another. Online forums, local gatherings, and spiritual retreats can provide opportunities to connect with like-minded individuals who can support and inspire you on your journey.

Practical Example: Join an online forum or a local magical group to connect with fellow practitioners. Share your experiences, seek guidance, and celebrate the magical journey together.

Honoring the Natural World
Nature is an abundant source of magical energy and wisdom. Take the time to commune with the elements, explore sacred sites, and listen to the whispers of the wind. Engaging in nature-based rituals, such as offering prayers or performing ceremonies, can deepen your connection to the magical forces that surround us. Remember to approach the natural world with reverence, gratitude, and respect.

Practical Example: Find a serene natural location, such as a forest, mountain, or beach, and spend time in quiet contemplation. Observe the beauty around you, meditate on the interplay of the elements, and allow nature to guide you on your path.

Embodying the Magic Within
Ultimately, the magic you seek resides within you. It is not merely an external force to be harnessed, but a profound connection to your own essence. Embody the teachings and practices you have learned. Let them become an integral part of your being. Live in alignment with your magical values, bringing the transformative power of the enchanted Himalayas into every aspect of your life.

Practical Example: Choose a magical practice that resonates with you and commit to incorporating it into your daily routine. It could be a meditation, a visualization exercise, or a mantra recitation. Embrace it as a way to infuse your life with magic.

The enchanted Himalayas have bestowed upon us a glimpse of their profound wisdom, but the path ahead remains uncharted. Embrace the never-ending quest with an open heart and a curious mind, for the magic of Tibet will continue to unfold before those who seek it. May your journey be filled with wonder, growth, and the joy of exploration. Safe travels, magical adventurer.

Made in United States
Cleveland, OH
19 June 2025

17827866R00036